9 Lessons from the Universe

SAMIE AL-ACHRAFI

Design by Anna Denardin and José Carlos Ferrari

Copyright 2022 © Samie Al-Achrafi

All rights reserved.

ISBN 978-18-380-6789-2

The Magic of 9

Why nine lessons? It all comes down to the extraordinary nature and properties of the number 9.

9 is considered the number of transformation, enlightenment and completion. It symbolises the maximum expression of possibility and wholeness – the culmination of wisdom and experience – in anticipation of new beginnings.

Let us take a moment to reflect on some of the mystery and meanings of this particular building block of the universe, looking at just a few of the many qualities that make it the perfect symbolic container for our journey.

- There are 360 degrees in a circle. Add 3 + 6 + 0 and you get 9. Cut the circle in half and there are 180 degrees – add these digits together and you get 9. Cut the semi-circle in half and there are 90 degrees in the quadrant – 9 again. We can continue with this division and the resulting angle will always reduce to the number 9.

● If you multiply any number by 9, then add the resulting digits together and reduce them to a single digit, that digit will always be 9. For example, 7 x 9 = 63; reduce 63 to a single digit by adding the digits together: 6 + 3 = 9. Similarly, 9 x 9 = 81, 8 + 1 = 9. Or 53 x 9 = 477, 4 + 7 + 7 = 18, 1 + 8 = 9. Any number, no matter how large, multiplied by 9 reduces to 9. No other number has this quality.

● When you add a single-digit number to 9 and reduce the result back to a single digit, it always reverts to the original number, as if nothing was added at all. For example, 6+9 = 15, 1+5 = 6; 8+9 = 17, 1+7 = 8; 1+9 = 10, 1+0 = 1.

So, 9 is all and yet nothing at the same time, depending on what we do with it.

May its magic and mystery power our explorations.

We must only begin; the rest will follow

Lessons

1. The Milky Way 14
2. Elements 22
3. Invisible Order 30
4. Life on Earth 40
5. Ecosystems 52
6. Humanity 62
7. Time 76
8. Perception 86
9. Brain 94

'A person who doesn't know what the universe is doesn't know where they are. A person who doesn't know what their purpose in life is doesn't know who they are or what the universe is. A person who doesn't know any of these things doesn't know why they are here.'

– Marcus Aurelius, *Meditations*

If I were to ask you, 'Who are you?', what would you say? What story would you tell?

For you to be alive, the universe has to be old enough for carbon to have been made in early generations of stars, and for planets to have formed, of which one was just the right size and distance from a star to give the perfect conditions for life to emerge. The chances of this are estimated to be 1 in 10 to the power 2,685,000. That's 10 with 2,685,000 zeros after it. Think of it like this: it is the probability of 2 million people getting together to play a game of dice in which every one of them rolls a trillion-sided die at the same time and they all come up with the exact same number.

Many of us no longer contemplate the deeper meaning of our existence or ask fundamental questions about it. But it's time to go back to the big questions, to feel again the wonder of who and what we are.

Studies of the workings of the natural world are enabling us to acquire more knowledge and make predictions that are radically altering our view of our place in the universe. Extraordinary scientific advances are greatly enhancing our ability to observe both the micro- and the macrocosmic worlds, offering us new perspectives on the underlying truth of reality.

At the same time, investigations into the nature of consciousness itself are also opening up new and sometimes bewildering vistas of enquiry into the limits of our perception, as well as how mind and matter might interact. This more developed scientific understanding provides an effective springboard for a new philosophical exploration of our journey in the physical plane.

'Look deep into nature and you will understand everything better.'

– Albert Einstein

Perhaps it is already inspiring the evolution we are currently experiencing in parts of our society, catalysed by the increasing numbers of people reawakening to such age-old but long-neglected questions as 'Who am I?', 'What is my purpose on Earth?' and 'What does it mean to be human?'

What follows are nine lessons from the universe. May they fill you with awe at the miracle that is your life.

1. The Milky Way

OUR GALACTIC HOME IN THE VASTNESS OF SPACE

The Milky Way contains billions of stars, but the sun is the only star in our solar system. The next closest stars to us are in the constellation Centaurus, about 40 trillion kilometres away. Given the time it takes for light to travel, we see these stars as they were four years ago.

The sun is at the centre of our solar system. It formed from gas and molecular clouds just over 4.5 billion years ago and is heated to incandescence by nuclear fusion reactions in its core, which radiates energy, mainly as visible light, ultraviolet light and infrared radiation. Its rays take eight minutes to reach our eyes, although what we can see of these rays actually comprises only 0.0035% of the electromagnetic spectrum. This boundless energy makes the star shine and it is by far the most important source of the energy that creates life on Earth.

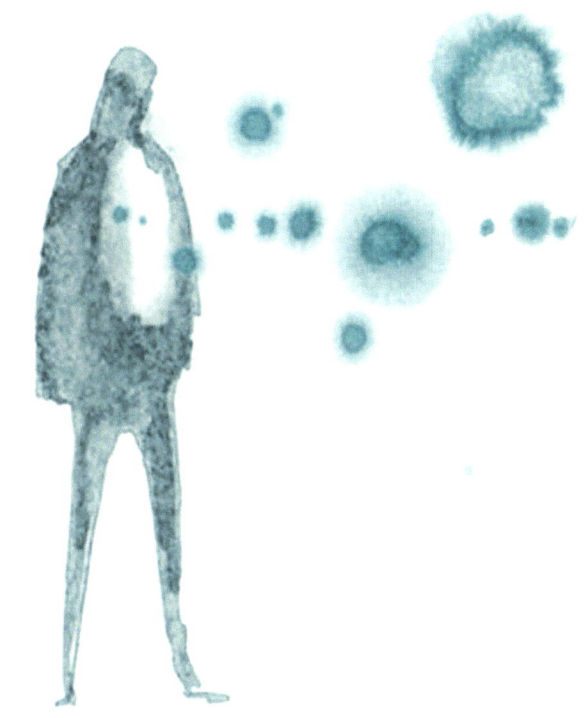

Which aspect of the world around you makes you shine?

For the first million years of its life, the sun was pretty much alone in our part of the Milky Way. Dust swirled around it, clumping into objects that grew to the size of pebbles, which then ground together over time and expanded to resemble boulders. It is believed that some of these broke apart, while others remained intact, gradually attracting more and more material to themselves, and becoming the building blocks of planets – named after the Greek word for 'wanderer'.

The planets in our solar system orbit the sun and, in turn, the solar system orbits the centre of the Milky Way galaxy, taking about 250 million years to revolve once around the galaxy's centre. This length of time is called a cosmic or galactic year. In the entire history of the human race, we have travelled less than 0.1% of that galactic orbit.

The remarkable images from the James Webb Space Telescope are allowing us to gain insights into new depths of the observable universe, yet its vastness is beyond comprehension, stretching more than 92 billion light years in diameter. Contemplating the immensity of the cosmos in which we find ourselves helps us to connect more deeply with the marvel of our human existence.

In this cosmic game of billiards, in one of the universe's trillions of galaxies, one of that galaxy's 200 billion stars wound up with a planet orbiting it at exactly the right distance for life to be sustained. And on that small, blue planet, a tiny part of the cosmos became conscious.

2. Elements

THE ETERNAL ALCHEMY OF BEING

Stars are very large accumulations of gases that release energy from nuclear fusion reactions. If you think about it, a star is essentially in a constant struggle. Gravity is trying to squash everything down, and as the star resists its collapse, elements of life are created through a series of stages.

Hydrogen is the lightest and simplest of all elements to fuse and release heat. In Stage 1, while there is still a supply of hydrogen to fuse, the star converts hydrogen to helium in the core. Vast amounts of energy are released, creating an outward pressure, which balances the force of gravity and keeps the star stable. Eventually, the hydrogen in the core runs out, at which point the fusion process stops, and the outward pressure ceases when energy is no longer being released. The star starts to collapse rapidly, leaving a shell of hydrogen and helium behind.

Beneath this shell, as the core collapses, the temperature rises again until Stage 2 starts, and helium nuclei begin to fuse together. Helium fusion releases more energy, which halts the collapse, and more elements, such as carbon and oxygen, are produced in greater quantities. This is where all the carbon in your body – in every living thing on the planet – was created: in the heart of an aging star.

Pressure shapes our lives too, catalysing the next stage in our growth

For massive stars, the fusion process does not end there. When the helium runs out, gravity takes over again and the collapse continues. The temperature rises once more, launching Stage 3, where carbon fuses into neon, sodium, magnesium, aluminium, among others.

And so it goes on. The core collapses, and this triggers the next stage of fusion, which creates heavier elements – each stage getting hotter and shorter than the last – until, eventually, the core is transformed into almost pure iron, and the fusion process stops.

Exactly how a star dies depends in part on its mass. It can collapse into various types of neutron star, form a black hole, or explode into a supernova – the explosion of a super-massive star, which spreads elements created during the life of the star far across the universe.

Whenever galaxies collide, this raw material gets brought together by the force of gravity. Intergalactic collisions result in a richer mix of elements, which become building blocks in stellar nurseries that trigger a new era of star and planet formation.

The destruction of something old opens the way for something new to emerge

Consider this: the iron in our bodies can only have come from the remains of a supernova. Without these previous generations of stars, all the iron contained in the Earth could not have been accumulated. And without that iron, we would be unable to move the blood that flows in every one of our heartbeats.

Right now, your heart is beating, pumping blood around your body. The haemoglobin in blood contains iron that transfers oxygen from the lungs to your tissues in order to nourish you – such that the 3 billion heartbeats of your life hold meaning.

We are the outcome of grand cosmic events. It turns out, we *are* made up of star stuff after all.

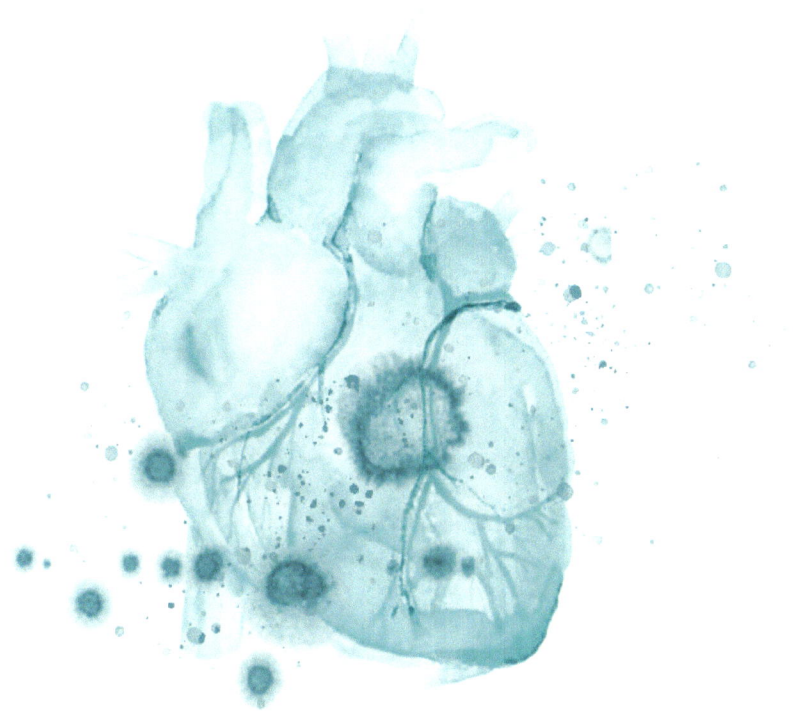

We are all connected through our hearts to a cosmic event

3. Invisible Order

PAY ATTENTION TO THE THINGS YOU DON'T NORMALLY SEE

The universe has no 'solidity' as such. At the most fundamental level, everything in it is pure vibratory energy manifesting itself in different ways. What we perceive as hard matter is mostly empty space with a pattern of energy running through it. In fact, everything is energy – the universe, our galaxy, the planet, us: organs, cells, molecules and atoms. Matter is merely energy vibrating at different frequencies.

Energy is all there is – vibration is the key

Atoms are what make up the matter we interact with every day. An atom is a positively charged nucleus orbited by negatively charged electrons with a great deal of empty space between them. Due to the strong repellent force generated by the protons when they move near to each other, the nuclei of atoms can never touch each other, unless they are fusing to create a new element. But even then, their electrons will not come together.

Take a look at your hand now – it appears solid, but it is actually a mass of energy vibrating. When you lie in bed tonight, the electrons within your body and those that make up your bed will repel each other. Thus, you will hover at an unfathomably small distance above your bed.

If you can never truly touch something, how is it possible that you feel the textures of an object? It is due to the electromagnetic repulsion between the electrons of your body and the object that you are sensing. Touch receptors in the skin send signals through to your brain, which creates the perception that you are physically in contact with the object, but in reality you are not.

Reality is not what it seems to our senses — the bigger picture is infinitely more complex

Human beings are made up of about 7 billion, billion, billion atoms. These atoms can be traced back to the very first moments of the universe and, as far as modern science is concerned, will exist until the end of time, because energy can neither be created nor destroyed. All energy fields are connected, constantly moving into form, through form and out of form.

And so, at a glance, our universe appears to be a chaotic place – an anarchy of atoms – but in actuality they are all following rules and creating coherent patterns. The complexity arises out of the seemingly infinite permutations of these underlying patterns in combination with the laws of nature as we understand them.

Patterns in nature are visible regularities of form found in the natural world, and these can sometimes be modelled mathematically. In 1202, Leonardo Fibonacci introduced the Fibonacci sequence to the Western world – a never-ending sequence starting with 0 and 1, such that each number is the sum of the two preceding numbers. The sequence starts 0, 1, 1, 2, 3, 5, 8, 13, 21, 34, 55, 89, 144 and so on. Sometimes referred to as 'nature's secret code', this sequence can be seen in action in flowers, which typically have 3, 5, 8, 13, 21, 34, 55 or 89 petals.

If we take the ratio of two successive numbers in Fibonacci's series, dividing each by the number before it, we find the following series of numbers: 1/1 = 1, 2/1 = 2, 3/2 = 1.5, 5/3 = 1.666..., 8/5 = 1.6, 13/8 = 1.625, 21/13 = 1.61538... The ratios of sequential Fibonacci numbers as they go up to infinity approach the golden ratio 1.6180339... represented by the Greek letter phi (Φ), which mathematicians use to calculate the golden spiral – a logarithmic spiral whose growth factor equals the golden ratio.

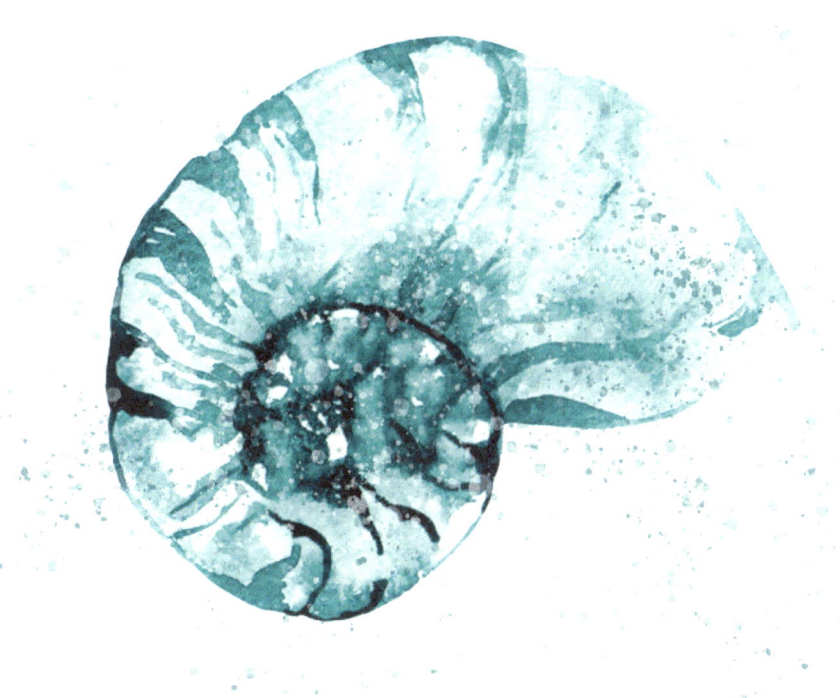

Patterns are codes to be read — what if we were to live our lives from this awareness?

The 'golden ratio' is a unique mathematical relationship and geometric expression that can be seen all around us in nature – the spiral of the nautilus's shell, the pentagonal form of some flowers, the arrangement of seeds in a sunflower, the flowering of an artichoke, an uncurling of a fern and the positioning of a pine cone's bracts.

The golden ratio has been called the 'divine proportion' because of the frequency with which it occurs in the natural world, but it is far from being the only pattern or rule underlying the structures of things. Different base patterns are thought to determine the appearance of animal spots and stripes, peacock feathers, honeycombs, meandering rivers and ripples in sand, to name but a few.

And yet within these patterns there is space for everyone and everything to bring its individual uniqueness. Consider the core template that gives form to snowflakes: each flake faces a different turbulent path through the atmosphere, each twist, turn and fall granting it a unique symmetry – just as happens with you.

There is an underlying order to everything and we are all unique expressions of it

4. Life on Earth

THE BIRTH OF THE BIOSPHERE

When Earth formed, there was no life. It emerged from the geology of an entirely inhospitable planet.

Liquid water is a prerequisite for life. It is theorised that asteroids and comets landed on the surface of primordial Earth, bringing with them the water that makes up our oceans. Recently, scientists have suggested that the sun's solar wind may also have played a part by turning dust grains into water.

The first living things were simple, single-celled microorganisms called prokaryotes, which have no cell nucleus or any other organelles (tiny structures inside cells that carry out specific functions) within them. Scientists believe they have discovered fossils of prokaryotic cyanobacteria cells dating back almost 3.5 billion years in Western Australia.

The Endosymbiotic Hypothesis proposes that eukaryotic cells – of which humans are made – evolved via a symbiotic relationship that developed between two prokaryotic microbes that merged. An anaerobic prokaryotic cell engulfed an aerobic prokaryote, which benefitted both – the larger cell was able to provide nutrients and protection, while the smaller cell was able to metabolise the nutrients and leverage oxygen to produce more energy. When the cells reproduced, they did so together, and over a long period of time the aerobes became mitochondria.

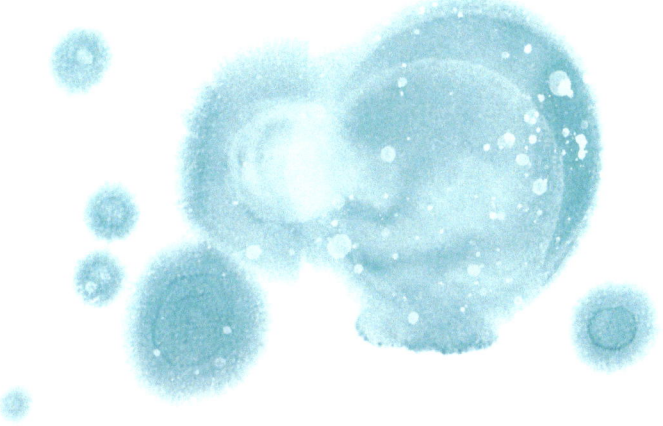

Life wants us to move forward as a collective. Which cooperation will transform you?

When cyanobacteria evolved, they set the stage for a remarkable transformation, becoming the Earth's first photosynthesisers. They made food using water and the sun's energy, and released oxygen as a by-product. It took a billion years for that oxygen to saturate the oceans before it was released into the air.

But even then, as oxygen appeared, the Earth immediately absorbed it. So the cyanobacteria had to work for another billion years, putting oxygen out until it started to accumulate in the atmosphere. This period in history is often referred to as the 'Boring Billion', marking a delay in the evolution of complex life, primarily due to low levels of oxygen in the atmosphere.

What in your life is calling for patience?

Around 600 million years ago, enough oxygen had accumulated in the Earth's atmosphere for the ozone layer to form, providing a vital protective shield from the ultraviolet light emitted by the sun. As conditions became more favourable, more complex organisms began to evolve.

Imagine that level of patience – all that time it took for complex multicellular life to proliferate in the seas, for plants to climb onto land, and the first animals to evolve and breathe the air, which ultimately paved the way for your life.

Nature is prepared to evolve. Are we?

To this day, mitochondria are the power stations found in the cells of every complex living thing. And yet once upon a time, these essential structures were separate, free-living creatures. For us to evolve, cells must have overcome their natural proclivity to replicate independently and started to cooperate as part of a larger entity. Just think about it: the mitochondria in your cells are descended from that single event in history.

Suppose you are one of those microorganisms – you are born into the world, live for a few weeks and then die. You might think nothing changed as a result of your life and that it didn't mean anything at all. But what you wouldn't have known is that you contributed to the possibility of countless life forms existing after you.

The ultimate purpose of our lives may not be obvious to us; it may even lie in a timeline beyond our current understanding.

We each have a greater role to play on Earth than our consciousness can perceive

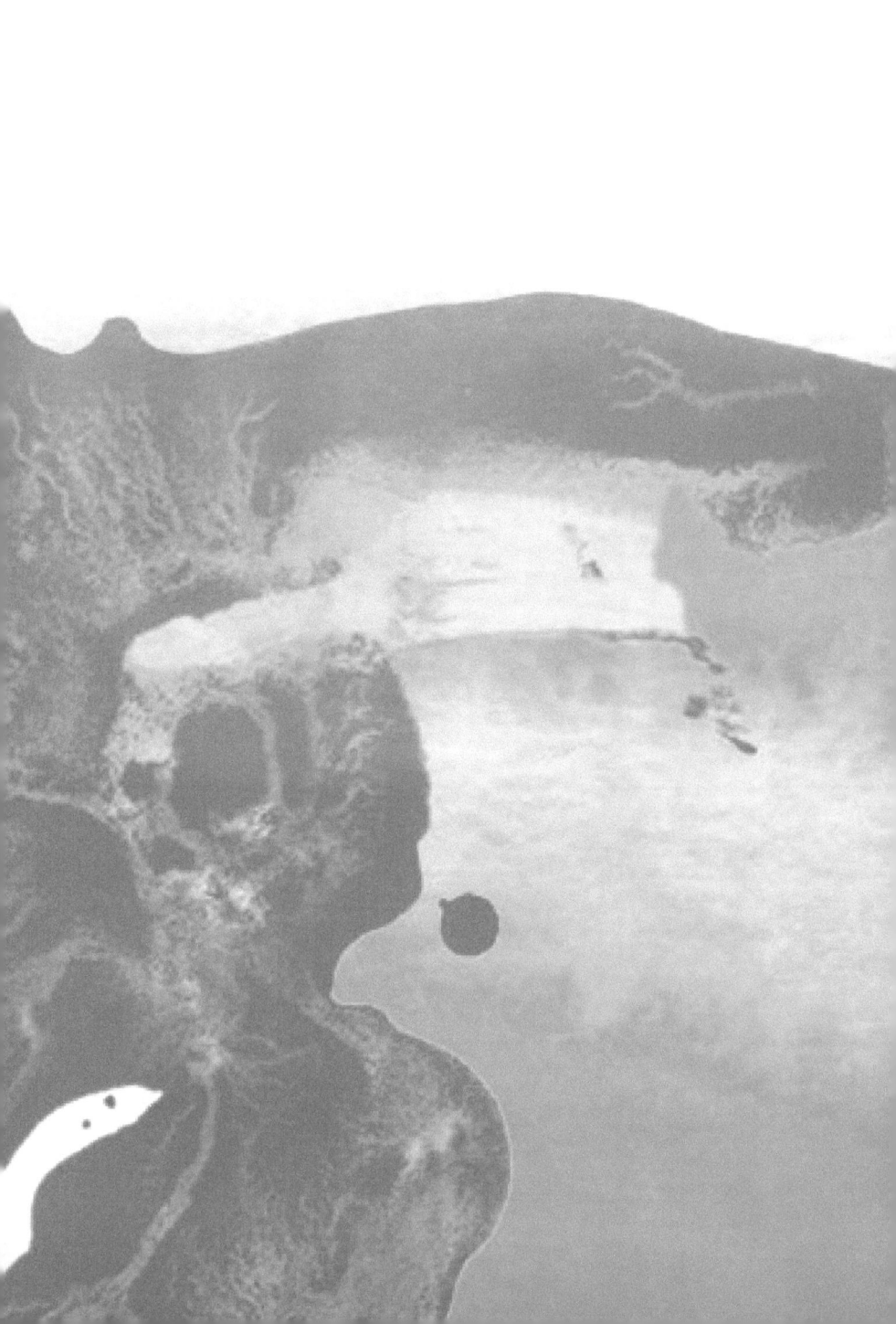

5. Ecosystems

THE INTERCONNECTEDNESS OF LIFE

What is life doing? In essence, it is metabolising energy from the external environment through a series of chemical reactions and making copies of itself. We use the oxygen we breathe to get energy from the food we eat, and that powers what goes on in all our cells – the common unit of life. The human body is made up of trillions of cells, all working together to give us the gift of life.

Cooperation is our natural modus operandi

All living things require a continuous supply of energy to sustain them, and all life forms depend upon each other – without plants, there would be no oxygen for us to breathe; without fungi, key organic material would remain locked in the ground. Through their metabolic processes and ultimately their death, animals return nutrients to the soil, ready to be made useful by bacteria and thus go around the cycle again. Just imagine: one teaspoon of healthy soil contains more microbes than there are people on the planet, and some 87% of all life on Earth depends on it. And so we see, some of the smallest things are responsible for some of the biggest cycles on our planet.

These tight, closed recycling systems took billions of years of evolution to create flourishing, complex ecosystems like forests and woodlands. They symbolise so much about our planet – incredible complexities that work together to maintain the wellbeing of the whole.

To perceive our interconnectedness on a grand scale, imagine sand and dust from the Sahara being picked up by the desert wind, lifted high into the air and transported across the Atlantic. The ocean receives part of this nutrient-rich sand, but as much as 40 million tonnes of it a year is carried all the way to the Amazon. Rain washes it out of the atmosphere and down onto the forests below, making Saharan sand a vital source of health and nutrition for the rainforest. The forest trees grow and take in carbon dioxide from the atmosphere, and breathe out oxygen through their leaves, acting as the lungs of our planet. In this way, the cyclical flow and the constantly swirling atmosphere sustain the cycle of life on Earth like a self-regulating organism.

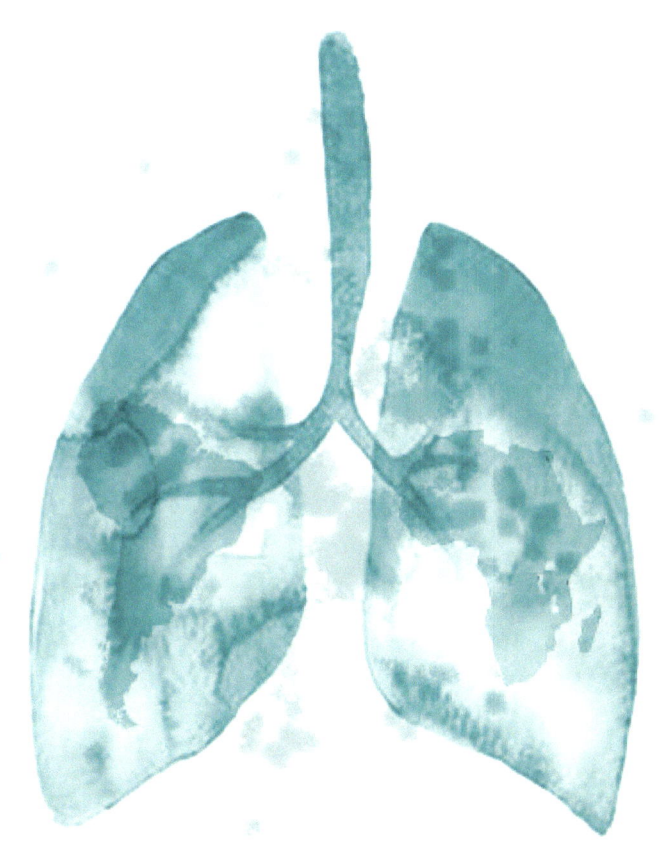

Take a deep breath.
Now consider: the air that fills your lungs may well have been on the other side of the planet last week

It is easy to take the air we breathe for granted. It is invisible, but we depend on it entirely – and on the plants that provide the oxygen we need. The atmosphere protects us from outer space and supplies us with oxygen to fuel our bodies. It is essential for all life, yet life itself created it.

Although some new atoms are added to Earth from cosmic dust and meteorites, the amount is not significant in relation to the entire mass of the planet. Therefore, Earth can be considered a closed ecosystem as far as matter is concerned.

The realisation that everything is connected within this ecosystem is leading to a renaissance of consciousness in which we see ourselves – and the structures we have created – as an integral part of a larger cyclical process of life. This is transforming how we perceive and interact with the natural world, enabling us to place ourselves back within the circular systems that restore and nourish Earth. These systems are continually working out their equally interconnected purposes, forming a mirror for the way our own individual purpose and mission are inextricably woven into the whole.

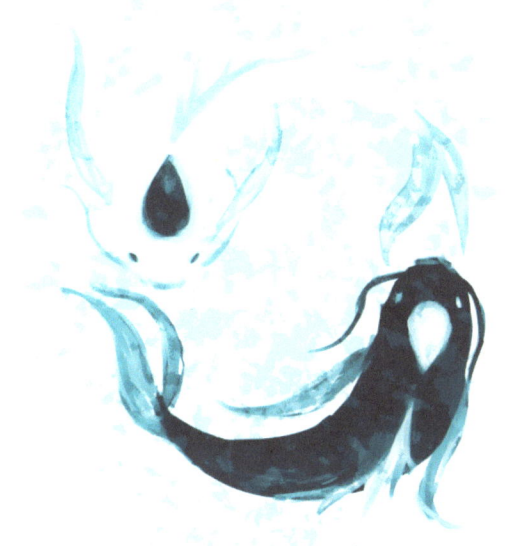

Nothing in nature exists for itself alone. The whole could not be whole without you

And as we connect back to this holistic sense of destiny, we see that our short existence on Earth is part of the overarching and unfolding story of our planet. From this follows the recognition that every human life is meaningful as an irreplaceable strand in the grand scheme of things.

The deeper sense of purpose we yearn for in our lives is inherently linked to our connection with and concern for the wellbeing of the entire planet and all its life forms, because we are an inseparable part of nature. In fact, we *are* nature.

We are evolving from ego-systems to ecosystems

6. Humanity

ONE HUMAN FAMILY

Two hundred and fifty million years ago the planet looked very different. All continents appear to have been connected in a supercontinent called Pangaea, meaning 'all lands' in Greek.

The theory of plate tectonics posits that Gondwana (the part of Pangaea composed of the land masses now forming Africa, South America, Antarctica, India and Australia) at some point split away from Laurasia (Eurasia and North America). About 150 million years ago, Gondwana broke up – India separated from Antarctica, and Africa and South America rifted. It was around 60 million years ago that North America split off from Eurasia.

Supercontinents are believed to have formed several times in Earth's history, only to be split apart before again coming together, in a cycle that lasts about 500 million years.

The current configuration of continents is unlikely to be the last. It is estimated that we are now about halfway through the present cycle and in another 250 million years a new supercontinent could form.

Our destiny is to come back together

The word 'homo', the name of the biological genus to which humans belong, is Latin for 'human', derived from the Indo-European root 'dhghem' for 'earth'. The genus emerged with the appearance of Homo habilis over 2 million years ago in Africa. Various other 'homo' species subsequently evolved on the same continent – among them, eventually, the first modern humans.

What happened when these creatures, gifted with large brains and the creative, imaginative, rational and emotional capacities of consciousness, were let loose upon the planet is plain to see in all the fruits of human activity – for better...and for worse.

Though we are a social animal, with a need to cooperate and organise ourselves collectively, we have also tended to suffer from opposing drives that cause us to splinter off from one another. One such divide is the idea of race. Most people think of racial difference as a natural phenomenon, but it is not a biological reality.

Each human cell contains around 6 feet of DNA. Let's say a human body has around 30 trillion cells – this would mean that each individual is carrying around 180 trillion feet of DNA. Approximately 99.9% of those 180 trillion feet of genetic code is the same in any two humans.

There is broad consensus across the biological and social sciences that race is a social construct, rather than an accurate representation of human genetic variation. In fact, genetic variation can be greater within groups typically considered to be part of a single 'race' than it is between 'races'. Notably, there is more genetic diversity within Africa than in the rest of the world put together.

In the stories we have created to foster and reinforce a sense of collective identity, we simultaneously created the idea of difference from those outside our own group. Myths shape our perceptions, almost from the moment of birth, leading us to think and behave in certain ways, and adhere to engrained cultural norms. Realising how these myths have coloured our worldview enables us to free ourselves from their sometimes-limiting beliefs – and the real-world consequences they carry.

We are all ultimately descended from the same ancestors

No matter how much we have ended up blinding ourselves to all that we have in common, we are driven by the same deeper urges; there is so much more that unites us than divides us. Beyond all the divisions put in place through the myths and narratives of the mind, we know that we are wired to be compassionate and to care for each other. Similarly, all the fear, anger and sadness that typically consumes much of our lives is widely shared in different forms across all divides.

We can use our awareness of this to return to a sense of our common humanity. And when we reconnect with a clear recognition of our shared aspirations and vulnerabilities, we can find the strength and intelligence to put our differences aside.

Can we come together with a common purpose — not to conquer or acquire more, but to evolve as beings, to become wiser and more loving?

The science is clear: our genes tell us we are one family, regardless of race or tribe. No one group can claim special status, because our origins – and our collective fate – are so deeply entwined. We are all, through more than 10,000 generations of ancestors, ultimately descended from someone who lived in the Rift Valley in East Africa hundreds of thousands of years ago.

You come from a long, unbroken line of ancestors who survived, in the face of adversity, at least to childbearing age. If you go back down this lineage, it soon becomes clear that the number rapidly increases, until statistical likelihood suggests you may have more in common with your neighbours than you think. You have two parents, four grandparents, eight great-grandparents, sixteen great-great-grandparents, thirty-two great-great-great-grandparents and so on down your ancestral line. By the time you get to your 262,144 great-

great-great-great-great-great-great-great-great-great-great-great-great-great-great-great-grandparents, you may well share at least one ancestor with someone you know who appears wholly unrelated to you.

The genes of your ancestors run through your veins, giving you a wellspring of inner strength and resilience

Ultimately, we can trace our origins back to the hydrogen atoms created at the beginning of time. In less than a quarter of a million years – one thousandth of 1% of the age of the universe – those atoms went from crafting stone tools to launching rockets into space.

As the stories we tell ourselves about our world and the universe unfold and develop, our awareness of who we really are is beginning to expand too, such that we may soon be living up to our name, 'Homo sapiens' – 'the wise ones'.

We think, work and dream together – now it is time to expand the concept of what it really means to be human, and care for each other too.

Your humanity to humanity could be your legacy

7. Time

A PERSISTENT ILLUSION

Earth has a unique set of natural cycles that we have used for thousands of years as a frame of reference to mark time and identify the events in our lives.

Although it feels as if we are motionless, the Earth rotates once on its axis every 23 hours and 56 minutes. We call this a day. One complete orbit of the sun takes 365 days, 5 hours, 59 minutes and 16 seconds, during which time Earth will have travelled 940 million kilometres. We call this a year.

Nature flows in cycles; humanity turned them into time

How often do we find ourselves thinking, 'If only there was more time'? Well, days on Earth are actually getting longer due to the moon's effect on our planet's rotation. Around 1.4 billion years ago – when the moon was closer and Earth's rotation was faster – a day was just over 18 hours. As the moon slowly drifts away from us, we gain on average 0.00001542857 seconds a year.

Time is so central to the human experience, yet we have only a partial understanding of it. In October 1971, as part of a scientific experiment, caesium-beam atomic clocks were flown twice around the world on aeroplanes, once eastward and once westward, and then the clocks were compared against others at the United States Naval Observatory. When reunited, it was found that the three sets of clocks disagreed with one another – the clocks that went eastward lost 59 nanoseconds, and the ones that went westward gained 273 nanoseconds. In effect, the people involved in the experiment aged different amounts. Time is not as straightforward, nor as self-evident, as it may seem.

Einstein's general theory of relativity explains why we don't all experience time in the same way. He argued that gravitational interaction does not come from a force called gravity, but instead through an interaction between a mass and the geometry of space and time where the mass is located. This causes time to tick differently for all of us, because objects with a lot of mass create a strong gravitational field.

The farther away you are from the Earth's surface, the faster time appears to go in relation to the time on the surface of the Earth. This effect is known as 'gravitational time dilation'. The stronger the gravity, the more spacetime fabric curves, and the slower time itself proceeds. In other words, time is relative: it is experienced differently by different individuals.

Notice the moments in your life when you lose all sense of time

This suggests we can free ourselves from the limiting beliefs we hold about time through how we choose to experience it. We can simply choose to keep our focus on the present moment that we are experiencing – moment after moment – rather than slipping into pondering on the past or projecting into the future. This endless present moment is the only thing that is real. Everything else exists only as a mental construct.

The present moment is all we really have

It appears that these notions, so foundational to how we experience the world, are not even fundamental properties of nature. Indeed, conceptions of space and time appear to break down completely in black holes at the point of singularity – the geometric point in space where the compression of mass is infinite density and zero volume – implying that there is a deeper level of reality in which neither space nor time exists.

We are beginning to see that how we perceive reality is, to some extent, illusory.

Facing reality means befriending uncertainty and ambiguity

8. Perception

A CHANGEABLE VIEW

Dimensions are essentially the different facets of what we perceive to be reality.

Beyond the visible dimensions of length, width and depth of objects, space and time can be combined into a fourth-dimensional 'spacetime' structure. Yet there could be many more dimensions hidden from view. In fact, the theoretical framework of Superstring and M-Theory posits that the universe could exist in ten or more dimensions.

Rather than treating fundamental particles such as quarks, electrons and photons as lumps of matter or energy, string theorists imagine them as vibrations. The various masses, charges and energies of particles arise from the harmonics of the oscillating 'string', a line that can extend in many dimensions. In simple terms, it is a hypothetical idea that purports to be a Theory of Everything, able to explain the fundamental microscopic aspects of reality and tie together different forces, particles, interactions and manifestations within the same framework.

If our universe is multi-dimensional, how many facets of the issues we face are we not yet able to see?

Discoveries in quantum physics are leading us to question the basic nature of reality and how we interact with it. Quantum particles, for instance, seem to have no definite properties prior to being measured, and how they appear to us seems to depend on how we choose to measure them.

Even light seems to know whether to behave as a particle or as a wave according to the circumstances. It sometimes exhibits the properties of a wave and sometimes exhibits the properties of moving particles, but never both properties at the same time. If you set up an experiment to measure its wave properties – such as passing the light through a prism – it behaves as a wave. If, instead, you try to measure its particle properties, it is similarly obliging. It is truly both, implying that reality is somehow created during the process of observation and that our intention can determine outcomes. Both the wave and the particle nature are accepted as being part of one model today (wave–particle duality), with the understanding that the exact nature of light is not describable in terms of anything that is known to exist.

Our dominant way of thinking in dualistic opposites blinds us to the underlying unity

We are reminded that what we do not know about the universe is far greater than what we do know. As human beings, we tend to limit our sense of the possible to what we can perceive or what our belief systems tell us is possible – but this shuts us into a very limited experience of the world.

What we deem to be correct now will almost certainly not be so in the future – just look at beliefs throughout history and how they have evolved. We are being called upon to let go of our need for control and certainty, to rethink our paradigms, and to move away from the fragmentation created by the old models of understanding towards the more holistic and multidimensional conceptions indicated by recent scientific thought.

When we are open to different perspectives, we welcome more possibilities into our lives

9. Brain

OUR OWN INNER UNIVERSE

The human brain is the most complex phenomenon in the known universe, containing around 100 billion neurons. A single neuron actually looks quite simple – a biological cell with numerous extensions that can transmit electrical signals. It is the system as a whole that resembles a hugely complex web of extension cords connected to each other. Each neuron may be connected to up to 10,000 other neurons, and these pass signals to each other via as many as 1,000 trillion synapses.

Your brain is a mini universe in constant evolution

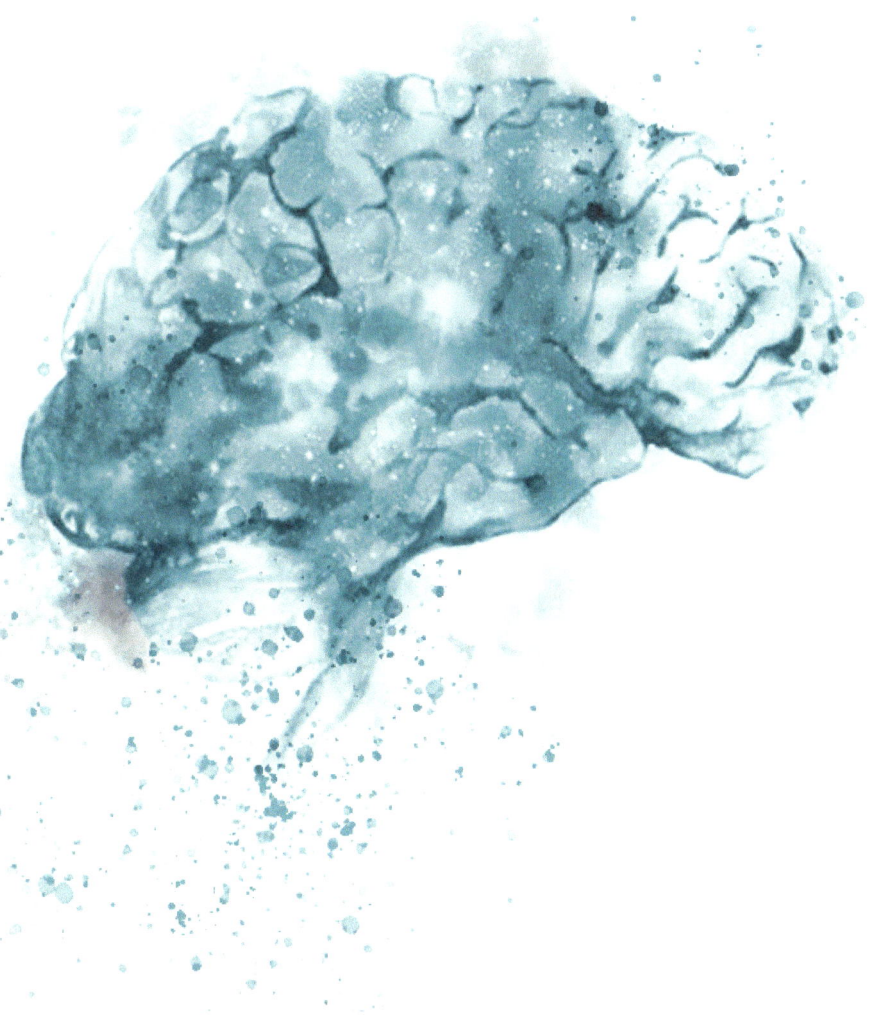

Cognition is the intricate polyphony of electrical signals between the brain's neurons – unique cells capable of processing information. It is estimated that the average person thinks around 50,000 thoughts a day, 95% of which are repetitive and 80% negative. Imagine what might be achieved, collectively and individually, if we were to alter this even slightly. We persist in looking outside ourselves for answers and solutions to everything, yet there is infinite potential latent within us.

The human brain is designed for learning – in fact, it is shaped by its own learning process. Neuroplasticity is the brain's ability to change in structure and function. If you have ever changed a habit or thought about something differently, then you have carved out a new neural pathway in your brain and experienced neuroplasticity. By repeatedly directing your attention towards a desired change, you can rewire your brain.

To be alive is to change— to change is to be alive

As the brain learns by changing its inner connections, so can we. When we describe 'a spark of creativity', it is quite literal – creativity is the process of solving a problem by creating a new pattern of connections, a spark between previously unrelated concepts. When we were children, we were naturally creative in this way, but the intellectual, logical, linear bias of society has stopped such sparks from flying so freely within our minds. What abundance of original ideas and inventive genius and inspiration have we excluded by cultivating only the rational mind?

It is time for us to move from believing ourselves to be experts to allowing ourselves to be explorers once again. And if we encourage the collaboration of diverse individuals with different brains, we can further extend the sparking process to generate the new ideas and values that are needed for collective resilience.

Your every thought has a frequency and emits a vibration into the world. If everyone were to imagine peace for a day, how might the world be changed?

It is this genuine, individualistic kind of diversity that we truly need to recognise and promote if we are to thrive. For all that we are essentially the same under the skin, we are nonetheless a magnificently diverse group of beings – and the more our approaches allow for and foster the maximum expression of diversity of thoughts and ideas, the greater our chances of finding innovative solutions to the issues of our time.

One way we may be able to reclaim more of the power that lies within our grey matter and use it to support our collective journey is revealed by explorations of our brainwaves. Brainwaves are categorised in terms of their frequency, measured in cycles per second using an electroencephalogram (EEG). Each of the basic EEG brain waves (delta, theta, alpha, beta, gamma) is linked to different states of consciousness and is useful for different skills and abilities. As our way of life and the related dominant modes of thinking have tended increasingly to keep us in one particular brainwave frequency at the expense of the others, we cannot always access the optimum type of brainwave for the activity at hand. By exploring our inner world, we can increase the accessibility and amplitude of desired states, making choices from expanded levels of consciousness to create our external reality.

You expand your abilities by expanding your consciousness

Neuroscientists at the University of Wisconsin-Madison have shown the impact of this by performing an experiment with two groups – meditators and non-meditators. Participants were brought into a laboratory and a metal plate was strapped onto their wrists, through which water could be circulated and the temperature regulated. The participants experienced very hot water once, so they knew what to expect. Then they were placed in an MRI scanner for the formal experiment and told they would hear one of two tones. A high-pitched tone meant that in ten seconds they would be zapped with this painful stimulus. If they heard a low tone, however, they should expect the water to feel just warm instead of unpleasantly hot.

As soon as the high-pitched tone was sounded, the brains of those in the non-meditating group responded as if they had received the painful heat, though they had only heard the tone.

With the meditators, nothing happened after they heard the tone – their pain matrix remained flat. When the heat came on, both groups responded, but when the heat went off again, the meditators came back to baseline, whereas the pain circuits of the non-meditators continued to reverberate. The conclusion: the increased levels of awareness of the meditators enabled them to respond more accurately to stimulus from the outside world, and thus not experience unnecessary pain.

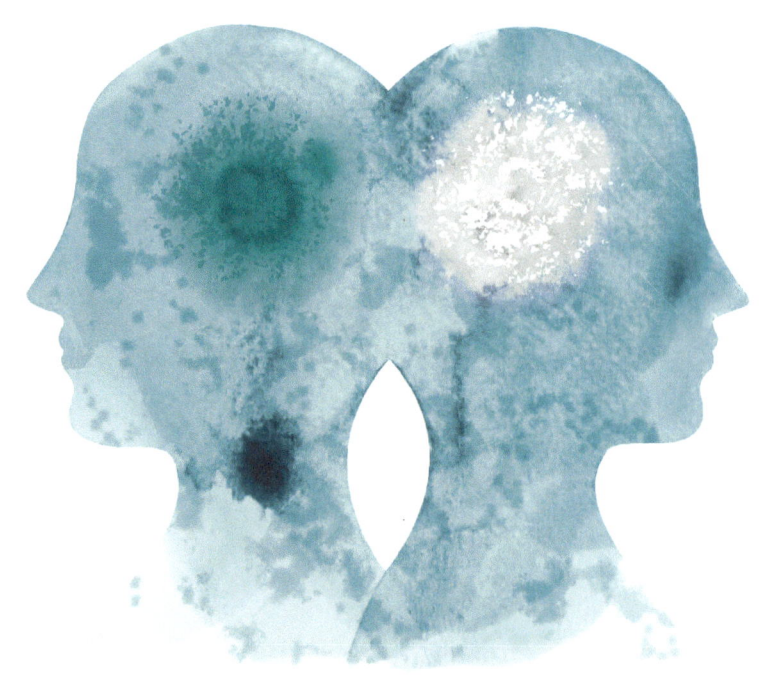

Your reality is constructed by your brain. What you give power to, has power over you

So much of what makes us who we are – our thoughts, character, emotions and values – can be seen to emerge from the electrical activity inside the 1.5 kilograms of matter housed in the cranium of every human that has walked the Earth.

But does it ultimately originate there? Any theory that relies exclusively on the nervous system to account for human minds and consciousness is surely incomplete. Modern science was designed to exclude consciousness, but nowadays many researchers are pointing towards the tantalising possibility that consciousness might even come from outside the mind and matter.

And so we see, the quest to understand the universe is the quest to understand who we are, and who we could be.

It's time to bridge the outer and inner worlds

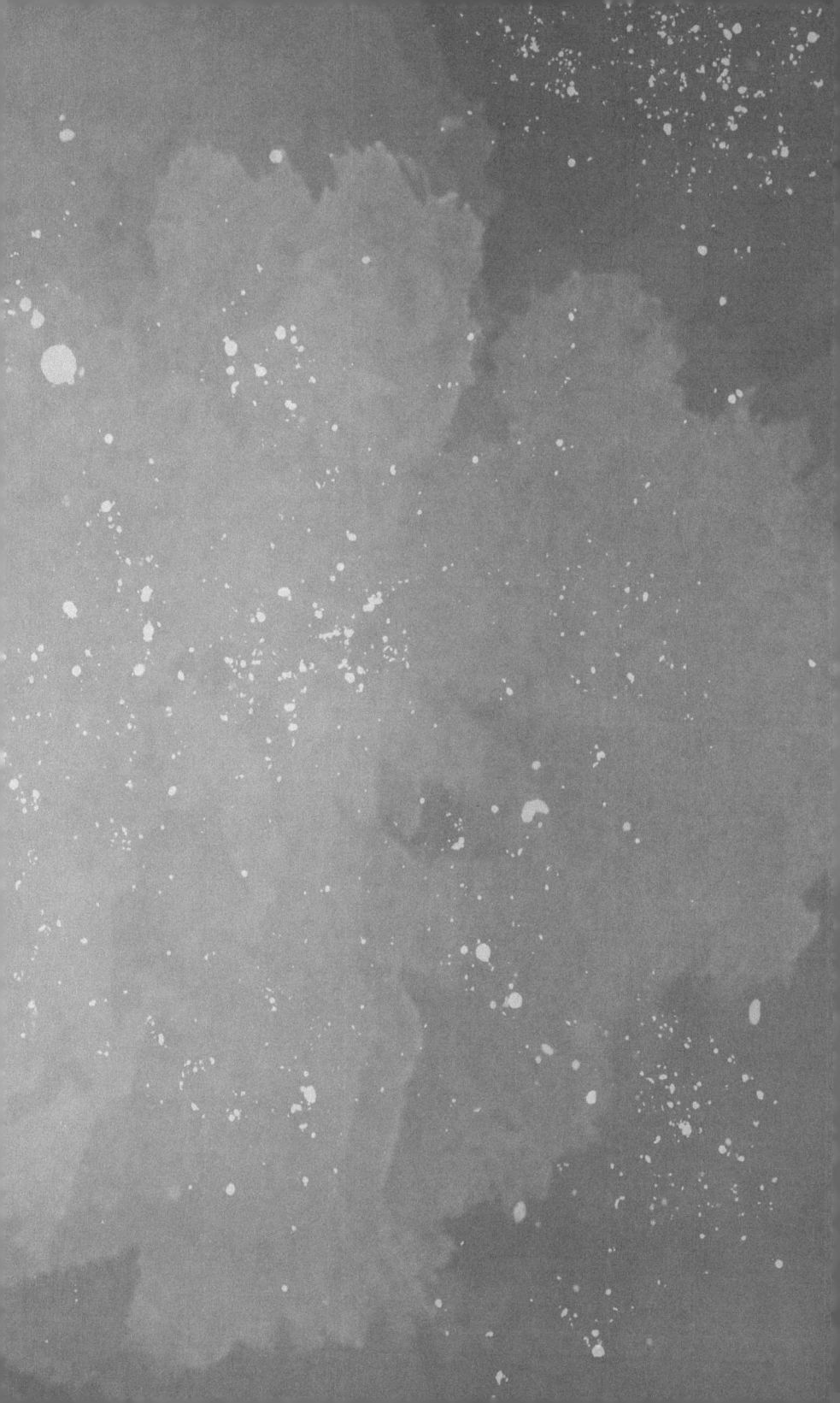

'Even if there is only one possible unified theory, it is just a set of rules and equations. What is it that breathes fire into the equations and makes a universe for them to describe? The usual approach of science — of constructing a mathematical model — cannot answer the questions of why there should be a universe for the model to describe. Why does the universe go to all the bother of existing?'

– Stephen Hawking, A Brief History of Time

We are a long way from fully understanding the mysteries of the universe, but we are beginning to lift the veil. Reimagining our place within it helps us to spin the thread of our life within the tapestry of humankind.

That we, with all our extraordinary and still largely unexplored potential, were born on a fragile ball of life hurtling through the vastness of space…could anything be more miraculous?

Tonight, look up at the stars. Keep your eyes turned skyward until you lose yourself in the sheer scale and majesty of it all. When you are ready to come back to now, to come back to Earth, take a moment to consider: this is our home, the only home we have, and the source of all that gives our lives beauty and meaning.

'We shall not cease from exploration
And the end of all our exploring
Will be to arrive where we first started
And know the place for the first time.'

– TS Eliot, 'Little Gidding'

On this journey of discovery, we should be aware that the lessons of science are experimental, and the scientific view of the world is a partial one that misses out aspects that cannot be grasped statistically. Who wrote the rules of the game – the origin of the cosmos and the laws of nature? How did life first come into being? Does consciousness underpin quantum physics, or is it the other way around? What happens to our souls when we depart our earthly vessels? Nobody has worked it out yet. It's up to you – what do *you* think?

What is certain is that everything and everyone

is interconnected. If that realisation is allowed to sink in, then a whole new way of being can take shape. Today, a series of once-in-a-lifetime meetings will happen that can never be replayed. As you go about your day, look into the eyes of someone you meet and know that your whole lives have brought you to this moment of now. After all, you both have your origins in a galactic event that occurred outside the solar system aeons ago.

We are now writing a new chapter in the human story, charting our path to a truer sense of our purpose and destiny. And with this knowledge comes responsibility.

It takes courage to flow in this new level of awareness, but the rewards are great. It is from these more conscious and enlightened ways of thinking that new leaders will emerge as we move towards a better future together.

It's #time4humanity.

So, if I were to ask you, 'Who are you?', what would you say? What story would you tell?

www.ingramcontent.com/pod-product-compliance
Ingram Content Group UK Ltd.
Pitfield, Milton Keynes, MK11 3LW, UK
UKHW060124240426
12049UKWH00012B/155